DISCOVERING THE UNITED STATES

South Dakota

BY IB LARSEN

Kids Core

An Imprint of Abdo Publishing
abdobooks.com

abdobooks.com

Printed in China.
052024
092024

Cover Photo: Shutterstock Images
Interior Photos: Dimitri Carol/Alamy, 4–5; Matteo Chinellato/Shutterstock Images, 7 (top left); Shutterstock Images, 7 (top right), 22, 26, 29 (bottom); Iryna Rasko/Shutterstock Images, 7 (bottom left); Sergey Demo/Shutterstock Images, 7 (bottom right); Photo by Mike Kline/Moment/Getty Images, 8; Philip Thurston/E+/Getty Images, 10; Bettmann/Getty Images, 12–13; Everett Collection Historical/Alamy, 14; Scott Olson/Getty Images News/Getty Images, 16, 18; Jacob Boomsma/Shutterstock Images, 20–21, 28 (bottom); Mark Newman/The Image Bank/Getty Images, 23; Nicholas Martinson/Shutterstock Images, 24, 28 (top right); Red Line Editorial, 28 (top left), 29 (top)

Editor: Laura Stickney
Series Designer: Katharine Hale

Library of Congress Control Number: 2023949370

Publisher's Cataloging-in-Publication Data

Names: Larsen, Ib, author.
Title: South Dakota / by Ib Larsen
Description: Minneapolis, Minnesota: Abdo Publishing, 2025 | Series: Discovering the United States | Includes online resources and index.
Identifiers: ISBN 9781098294120 (lib. bdg.) | ISBN 9798384913399 (ebook)
Subjects: LCSH: U.S. states--Juvenile literature. | South Dakota--History--Juvenile literature. | Midwest States--Juvenile literature. | Physical geography--United States--Juvenile literature.
Classification: DDC 973--dc23

All population data taken from:
"Estimates of Population by Sex, Race, and Hispanic Origin: April 1, 2020 to July 1, 2022." *US Census Bureau, Population Division*, June 2023, census.gov.

CONTENTS

Sue the *T. rex* stands 13 feet (4 m) tall at the hip and is more than 40 feet (12 m) long.

Sue the Dinosaur

It was August 12, 1990. Scientists were exploring a cattle ranch in South Dakota. They were looking for **fossils**. The scientists had found a few dinosaur bones. They were ready to leave the ranch. But one scientist decided to take another look around.

Her name was Susan Hendrickson. She noticed some bones sticking out of a cliffside.

Soon Hendrickson's team realized that the bones were from a *Tyrannosaurus rex* (*T. rex*) dinosaur. People had found *T. rex* bones before. But nobody had ever found this many bones from a single *T. rex*. The team carefully dug

How Did Sue's Skeleton Become a Fossil?

Scientists think Sue died near a river. The river covered the dinosaur's body with sand and mud. That is why most of Sue's skeleton became a fossil. Sue's skeleton is about 90 percent complete. Most dinosaur fossils that scientists discover are not as complete as Sue's.

South Dakota Facts

DATE OF STATEHOOD
November 2, 1889

CAPITAL
Pierre

POPULATION
909,824

AREA
77,116 square miles
(199,730 sq km)

STATE BIRD

Ring-necked pheasant

STATE TREE

Black Hills spruce

STATE FLOWER

American pasque

STATE ANIMAL

Coyote

Each US state has a different population, size, and capital city. States also have state symbols.

the bones out of the cliffside. They named the skeleton Sue, after Hendrickson's nickname.

Many groups fought over who should have Sue. So the US government made a decision.

The Black Hills region is known for unique rock formations, such as the Needles. These tall, thin rock spires are a popular tourist sight.

It allowed the owner of the ranch to sell the fossil. In 1997, a museum in Chicago, Illinois, bought Sue for $8.4 million. Today, people can visit the museum to see Sue. But South Dakota was Sue's home for millions of years.

Land and Wildlife

South Dakota is in the US region known as the Midwest. It is a **landlocked** state. It borders North Dakota to the north. Nebraska lies to the south. To the west are Montana and Wyoming. East of South Dakota are Minnesota and Iowa.

South Dakota's land includes mostly grasslands with few trees. Bison and prairie dogs live throughout these grasslands. The Black Hills are in the western part of the state. This mountainous region is covered with forests. The area is home to deer, bobcats, and coyotes.

In the winter, people can see frozen waterfalls in Spearfish, South Dakota.

Climate

South Dakota has four seasons. The state is known for its extreme temperatures. Its winters are very cold, and its summers are very hot.

South Dakota gets less rain than most other states. Most rain comes during the summer. In the winter, South Dakota gets a lot of snow.

Further Evidence

Look at the website below. Does it give any new evidence to support Chapter One?

South Dakota

abdocorelibrary.com/discovering-south-dakota

Russell Means, *front row left*, was one of the leaders of the American Indian Movement (AIM). The group fought to protect American Indians' rights.

The People of South Dakota

The first people in South Dakota arrived around 10,000 years ago. Over time, American Indian nations emerged. These included the Mandan and Arikara. The Dakota, Lakota, and Nakota peoples also called South Dakota home.

During the Black Hills Gold Rush, many people came to South Dakota in search of gold. They created mining towns such as Deadwood.

These three nations are sometimes called the Sioux. South Dakota is named after the Dakota people. Today, the state recognizes nine American Indian nations.

In 1742, French settlers came to South Dakota. Few white Americans and Europeans lived in the region until the late 1800s. In 1874, settlers found gold in the state. Many people from eastern states traveled to South Dakota. They hoped to become rich by mining the gold. During this time, **immigrants** also came to the state. Many were from Germany, Russia, and Norway.

Pine Ridge Reservation

The Pine Ridge **Reservation** is in southwestern South Dakota. The land belongs to the Oglala Lakota Nation. It is one of the country's largest reservations by area. It has 4,353 square miles (11,274 sq km) of land.

Many rodeos are held throughout South Dakota, such as the Black Hills Roundup. Participants compete in events such as saddle bronc racing.

Several famous people have lived in South Dakota. Author Laura Ingalls Wilder lived in the state from 1879 to 1894. American Indian activist Russell Means was born in South Dakota in 1939.

Today, 81 percent of South Dakotans are white. Nine percent are American Indian, and 5 percent are Hispanic or Latino. Almost 3 percent of South Dakotans are Black. Asian people make up 2 percent of the population.

Culture

Immigrants brought unique foods to South Dakota. One is chislic. Germans and Russians likely introduced it. It features cubes of meat on skewers. Germans brought kuchen to South Dakota. This is a fruit pie topped with custard.

Sports are another part of South Dakota's culture. The state sport of South Dakota is rodeo. This sport was first practiced by cowboys in the United States and Mexico.

South Dakota is one of the country's top producers of corn.

Rodeo **contestants** compete in events. These include riding a bull or catching a calf with a rope. Judges give contestants scores based on their speed or skill. Dozens of rodeos are held every year in South Dakota.

Industry

Many South Dakotans have jobs in farming. People grow crops such as corn, soybeans, and wheat. Other farmers raise cattle, pigs, and turkeys. Many South Dakotans work in stores and hospitals. Tourism is another big industry. Many South Dakotans have jobs performing services for the state's visitors.

Explore Online

Visit the website below. Does it give any new information about the history of South Dakota that wasn't in Chapter Two?

Native Americans in South Dakota

abdocorelibrary.com/discovering-south-dakota

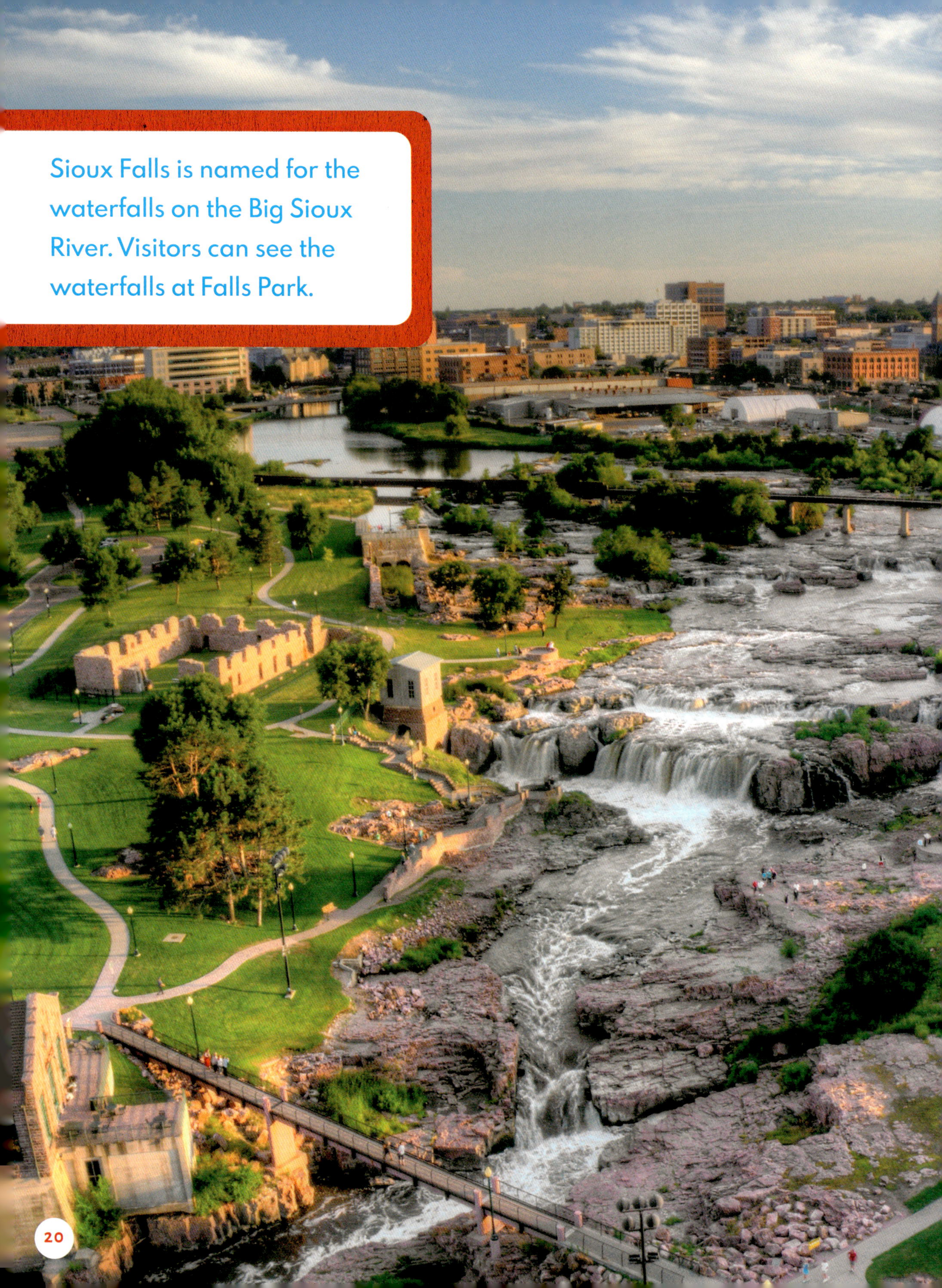

Sioux Falls is named for the waterfalls on the Big Sioux River. Visitors can see the waterfalls at Falls Park.

Places in South Dakota

South Dakota's capital is Pierre. But Sioux Falls is the state's largest city. More than 200,000 people live there. More than half of South Dakotans live in cities. These include Rapid City and Brookings. The state also has nine American Indian **reservations**.

Badlands National Park is home to many colorful rock formations and canyons. Visitors can explore trails and learn about how different rocks formed.

The Pine Ridge and Cheyenne River Indian reservations are the largest.

Parks

South Dakota has two national parks. One is Badlands National Park. Prairies cover the land. The park also has unique landforms, such as **buttes**. Visitors can hike and drive through the park. They learn about fossils discovered there.

Wind Cave National Park is a popular place for wildlife watching. Visitors can see animals such as bison.

At Wind Cave National Park, people can see a large underground cave. This cave formed hundreds of millions of years ago. Visitors can take guided tours through the cave. They can also explore aboveground.

Visitors to the park can hike through a prairie. They can see many different animals. These include bison and elk.

Mount Rushmore includes the faces of US presidents George Washington, Thomas Jefferson, Theodore Roosevelt, and Abraham Lincoln, *left to right*.

Landmarks

Mount Rushmore is one of South Dakota's most famous landmarks. It is a huge sculpture of the faces of four US presidents. The faces are carved into a mountainside. More than 2 million people visit the **monument** each year. Mount Rushmore has become a US symbol.

Near Mount Rushmore is a mountain carving of Crazy Horse. He was an Oglala Lakota chief. Crazy Horse led attacks against white settlers on Sioux land in the mid-1800s.

Artists started building the sculpture in 1948. It remained in development in the early 2020s. The completed sculpture will show Crazy Horse pointing forward while riding a horse.

Six Grandfathers

Mount Rushmore got its name in 1885. But long before that, the Lakota people named the mountain the Six Grandfathers. The Lakota consider the mountain and its surrounding land **sacred**. The six grandfathers are north, south, east, west, above, and below.

South Dakota's flag features the state seal. It includes images of a farmer, a river, and a steamboat.

There are many interesting things to do in South Dakota. Visitors can explore national parks. They can see rodeos. Or they can visit Mount Rushmore. South Dakota has something for everyone.

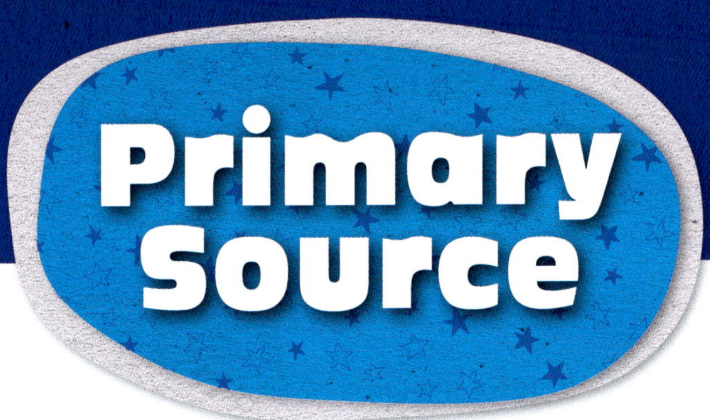

Mary Carpenter works in a fossil lab at Badlands National Park. She says:

> Badlands National Park is actually one of the richest fossil areas in the world. . . . We have things like mosasaurs, ammonites, and other marine animals. Any marine shallow sea type animals that you can think of."

Source: Catherine Maher. "'One of the Richest Fossil Areas in the World': Badlands National Park Fossil Preparation Lab." *NewsCenter1*, 19 June 2023, newscenter1.tv. Accessed 3 Nov. 2023.

What's the Big Idea?

What is this quote's main idea? Explain how the main idea is supported by details.

State Map

KEY

Point of interest

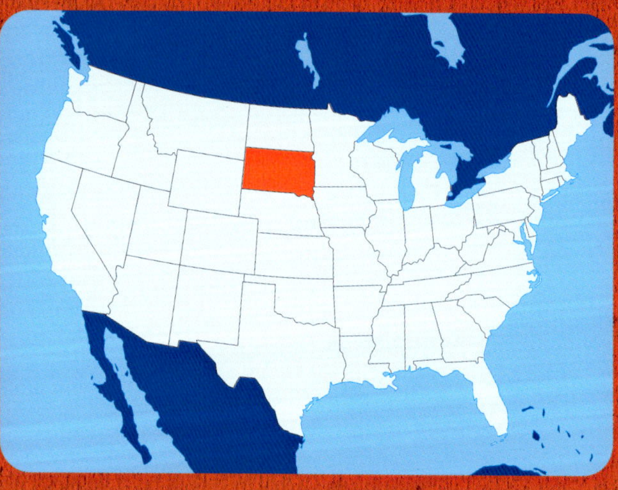

Mount Rushmore

South Dakota: The Mount Rushmore State

North Dakota
Montana
Wyoming
Minnesota
Iowa
Nebraska
N
W
E
S
Grand River
Lake Oahe
Aberdeen
James River
Big Sioux River
Deadwood
Rapid City
Black Hills
Mount Rushmore
Pierre
Brookings
Palisades State Park
Sioux Falls
Badlands National Park
White River
Crazy Horse Memorial
Pine Ridge Area Chamber of Commerce
Wind Cave National Park
Wounded Knee National Historic Landmark
Missouri River

Badlands National Park

Glossary

buttes
hills with steep sides and flat tops

contestants
people who compete in a contest

fossil
the very old, preserved remains of an animal or plant

immigrants
people who move to a different country

landlocked
describing an area that is entirely surrounded by land

monument
a structure built to remind people of a person or event

reservation
land set aside by a government for a specific group of people

sacred
having religious importance

Online Resources

To learn more about South Dakota, visit our free resource websites below.

Visit **abdocorelibrary.com** or scan this QR code for free Common Core resources for teachers and students, including vetted activities, multimedia, and booklinks, for deeper subject comprehension.

Visit **abdobooklinks.com** or scan this QR code for free additional online weblinks for further learning. These links are routinely monitored and updated to provide the most current information available.

Learn More

Bird, F. A. *Sioux*. Abdo, 2022.

Tieck, Sarah. *South Dakota*. Abdo, 2020.

Walker, Cameron. *National Monuments of the U.S.A.* Wide Eyed, 2023.

Index

About the Author

Ib Larsen is a writer and editorial assistant living in Saint Paul, Minnesota.